CU00807494

We Can Sing
A Rainbow

To Mrs Smith,

Thank you for caring about us.

from

Everyone at Quince Tree.

13·11·97.

By the Pupils of

QUINCE TREE SCHOOL, TAMWORTH

*The School would like to thank the following
Companies for their financial assistance in the
production of this book*

FRESH EXPRESS
CHILLED DISTRIBUTION
Tel: (01827) 312426

SMURFIT RECYCLING
Tel: (01827) 66602

PRINTED & PUBLISHED BY:
WINE PRESS, 1 SILVER STREET, TAMWORTH
01827 67622

Quince Tree School, Tamworth
July 1996
ISBN 1 899705 75 9   £3.00

'To Teach is to Touch a Life for Ever'

This is the quotation above my desk which reminds me daily of what a privilege it is for all the staff at Quince Tree School to be able to play such a role in the lives of all our Special children. I sometimes think that the quote should read, *The Special Child Touches our Lives for Ever*, as each day we have the pleasure to share in their milestones of achievement and it gives me great pleasure to share with all of you this book which gives you an insight into their very special world.

We would like to dedicate this book to two of our very special pupils, John-Peter and Dawn who we will never forget.

V.A.Ver——.

V.A. Vernon
Headteacher.

Our Favourite Songs

I like to sing
"He's got the whole world in his
hands."

David Bull

"The wheels on the bus go
round and round.
All day long"

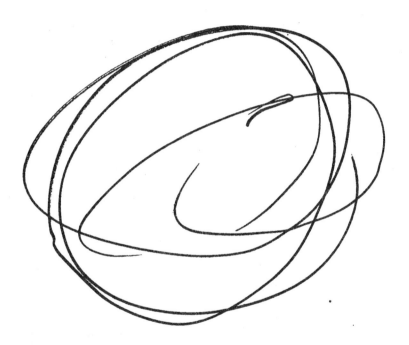

Kimberley Fulbrook

Paul Lynch

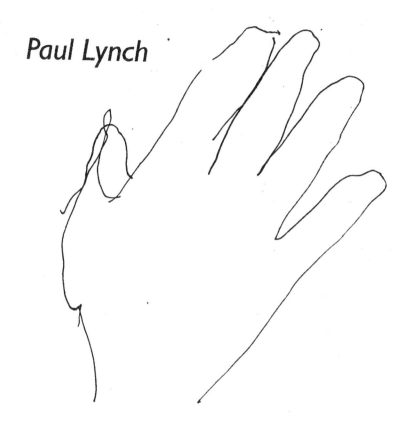

I use my hands to do the actions
when we sing
 "wind the bobbin up"
(Written by Becky)

Old MacDonald Had a Farm

farmer   farm

tractor

pig

Liam Farnsworth

I like to sing in music. My
favourite song is Kum bah yah.

Laura Chapman

I have got an Elvis Presley
c.D. I play it loud. I sing
and dance to the music I
play the drums. I have got
two sticks.
"stop playing so loud James,"
says mom .

James Rogers

"Say hello to Richard - hello,
hello Won't you let me hear you
say Hello, hello, hello"

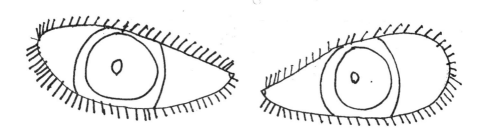

Richard can blink to say 'hello'

Richard Melling

"Roly poly, roly poly round and round"

Curtis Shakeshaft

I enjoy Playing Happy,
Birthday on the Piano at
assembly on Friday.
mornings. It Makes.
the children Happy.
Everyone thinks I'm very.
good at it.

IF I make a wrong note
I get cross with the.
Piano IF I play it right
I'm
            STEPHEN

Stephen Reynolds

I listen to my tapes every day. My favourite is 'The Muppets'. This is Gonzo.

Craig Berrow

I Can Sing a Rainbow

Laura Jordan

At School

At school I play on the swings with Chris.

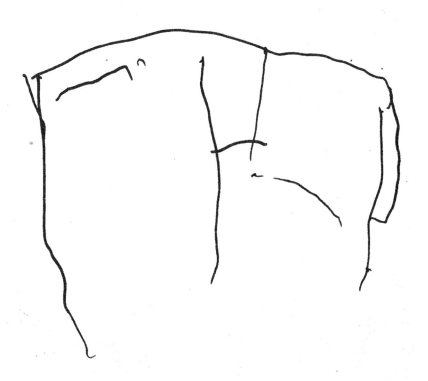

Leigh Stribling

AT QUINCE TREE SCHOOL I am in THE FE group and on wednesdays I go TO Tamworth COLLAGE we do LOTS OF different activities The one I chose was a food hygene course we had TO Learn LOTS of different rules about working with food IT was very hard work at The End of The course we, had TO do an exam I scored 18 POINTS OUT OF 20 SO I passed I am The first person at quince TO do This

Denise

Denise Perry

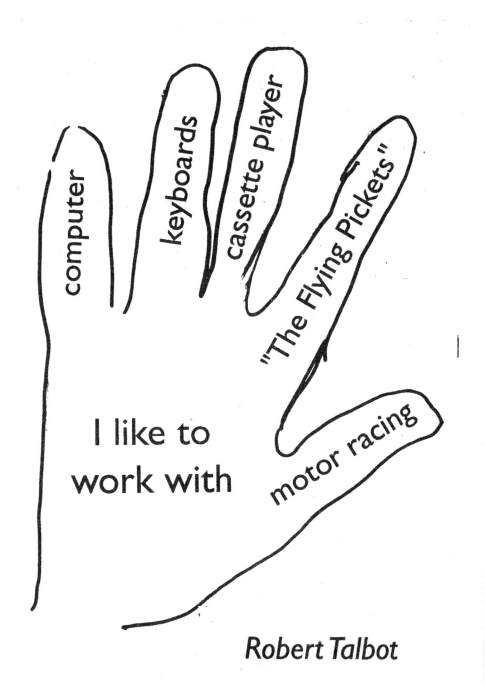

computer

keyboards

cassette player

"The Flying Pickets"

motor racing

I like to work with

Robert Talbot

Margaret helps me at school.

James Grice

Sue   Jo   Liz   margaret   Colin

School

I like Painting

I like writing

I like maths

I like drama

I like DaT

I like science

I love school.

kirk Claire me

Natalie

Natalie Scarrott

"I like to have my hands

massaged."
(Written by Joanne)

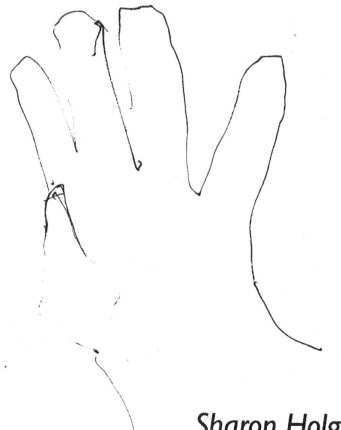

Sharon Holgate

I enjoy learning
French I can say
Bonjous which meohs Hello
I can also say Auevise
which me on I went to visit
goobye when I spoke french
france I spoke french this
people and the could uindstand
uhat I sord

David

David Sampson

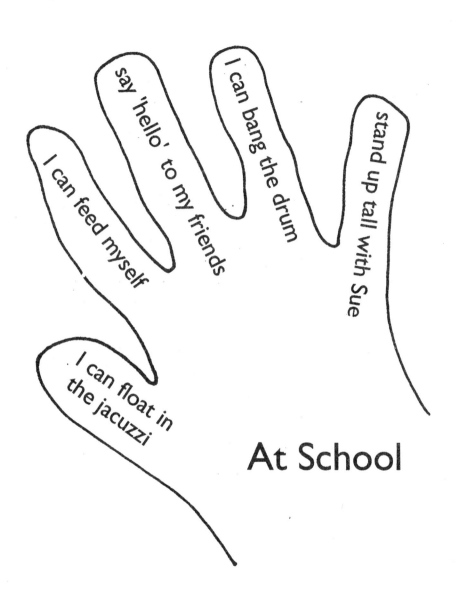

say 'hello' to my friends

I can bang the drum

I can feed myself

stand up tall with Sue

I can float in the jacuzzi

At School

Nathan Moseley

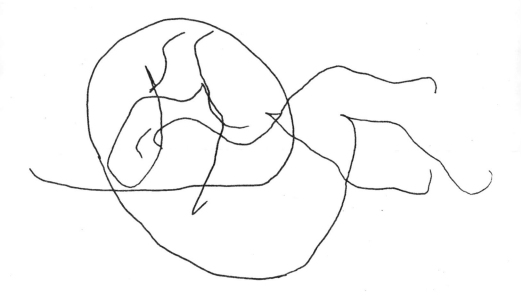

This is a picture of Sam enjoying his swimming lesson.

Sam Peers

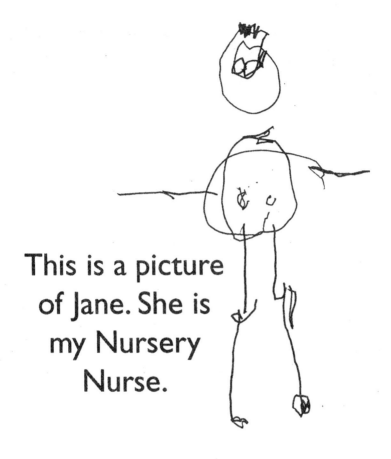

This is a picture
of Jane. She is
my Nursery
Nurse.

Katie Aucote

Katie Hembrow

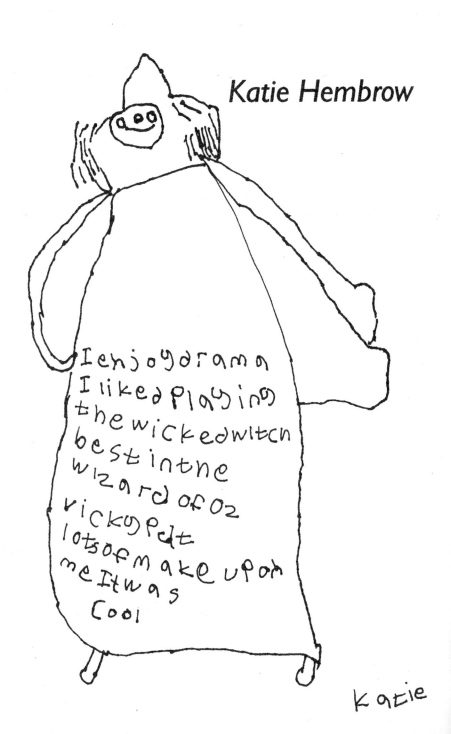

I enjoy drama
I liked playing
the wicked witch
best in the
wizard of oz
Vicky put
lots of make up on
me It was
cool

Katie

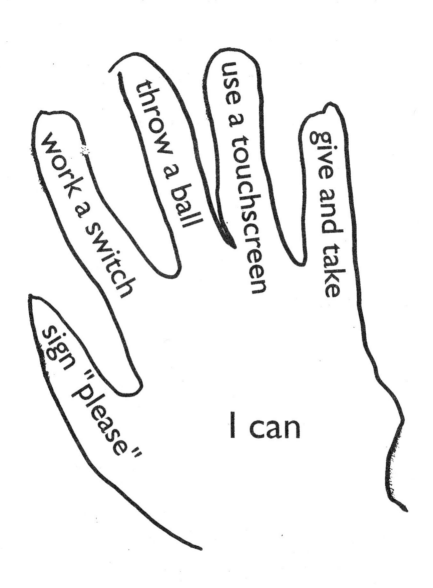

work a switch

throw a ball

use a touchscreen

give and take

sign "please"

I can

Mark Olden

I like going to school. I enjob English and Maths.

Samantha Pierce

Samantha Pierce

I love cooking my dinner at school.

I love beans on toast and an apple for my pudding.

John O' Donnell

This is my school.

I like P.E. and swimming.

I like chips for dinner.

SDROh

Sarah Pitts

Feeling & Feelings

A Happy Poem
Holidays

cara vans
Near the beach
I do the gardening
A different bed
It's sunny
Fish and chips.

claire

Claire Smith

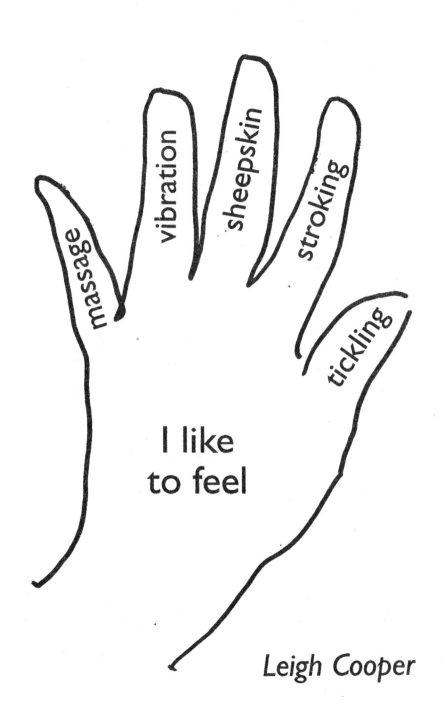

massage

vibration

sheepskin

stroking

tickling

I like
to feel

Leigh Cooper

It was good going to the
Clothes show at the N.E.C..
The male Modes were gorgegeous
I had my phototaken with them
I wish I could be a MODEL.

BECKY

Becky Pratt

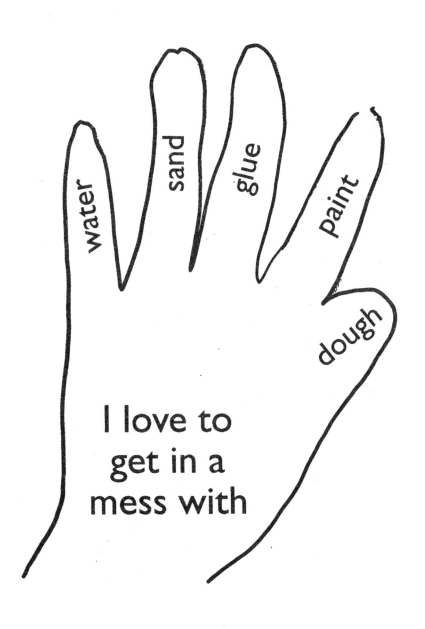

water

sand

glue

paint

dough

I love to
get in a
mess with

James Kelly

Tammy

Sue

Tammy is sad because
someone is naughty.
Sue is happy because
Jason is good.

Jason Clay

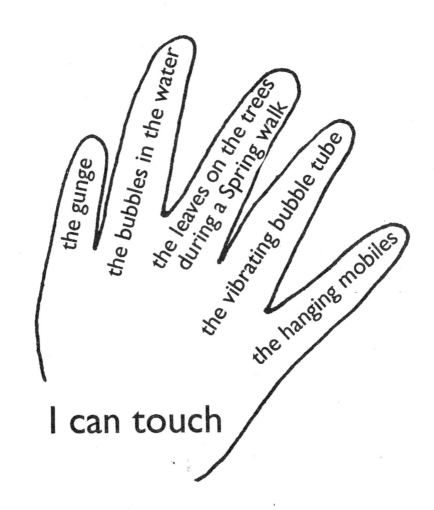

the gunge

the bubbles in the water

the leaves on the trees
during a Spring walk

the vibrating bubble tube

the hanging mobiles

I can touch

Jade Nash

A Sad Poem

The waterpark

The water is orange
The water The trees
were dead The fish

were dead

COLIN

Colin Davies

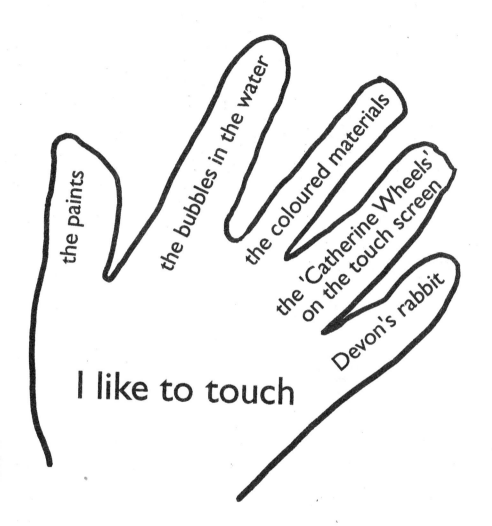

the paints

the bubbles in the water

the coloured materials

the 'Catherine Wheels' on the touch screen

Devon's rabbit

I like to touch

Matthew Kibble

The Queen vic

Happiness is

computer games
Eastenders
washing up

playing football

Riding on my bike

Horse Riding

Matthew Fox

I liked dancing at the Disco

It was good going to the Edge

Night club and dancing on the

podium I wore my best clothes

Kate

Kate Williams

Our Families

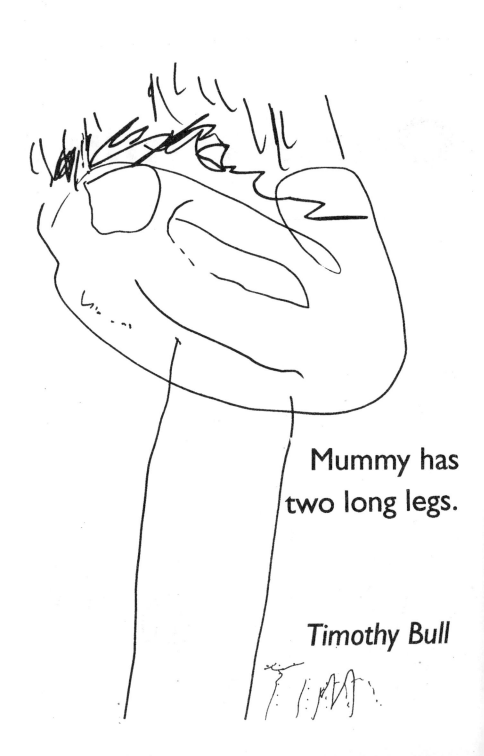

Mummy has
two long legs.

Timothy Bull

My Mum helps me at swimming.

Sean Carroll

Richard Brotherton

I go to visit my Nan. She lives at the pub.

Chris Dorman

I like playing with the puppets, this is the 'Daddy' puppet.

Lee Grieves

Dad

RYAD

Me

Mom

Mitchell Layton

Daddy and the dinosaur.

Claire Griffiths

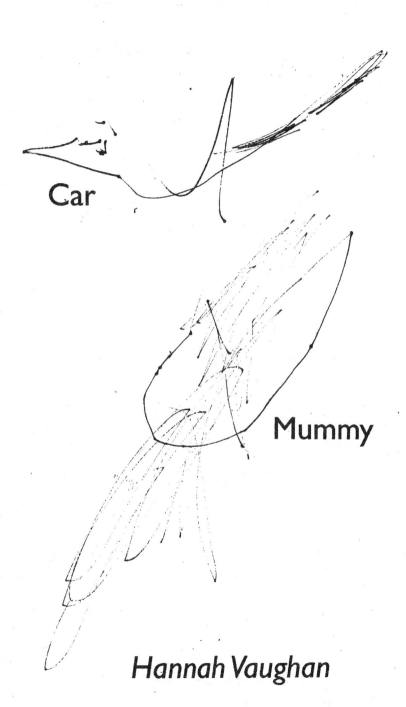

Car

Mummy

Hannah Vaughan

I like watching videos with my brother mark and my brother Richard our favourite video is snows white

Tammy Brotherton

Mommy

Daddy

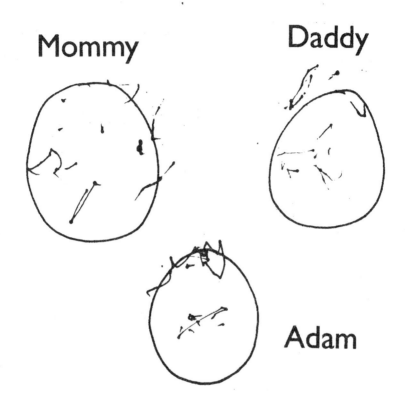

Adam

My Family

Adam Minshull

I like going to parties with my family, especially if there are balloons there.

Donna Allen

I Wish ...

I wish
I wιsɔh

I wish I was in Benedorm with my Mum
I wish I was inbenedormwienmymum

and Dad. It would be Summer. I would
and Dad It would be summer Iwou
15

watch T.V. I would go to the sea and
watchTV I woua go to the sea and

have a paddle. I would eat beans, sausage
haVe a paddle I woulbeat beans sausage

and stuffing. I would eat ice-cream and Jelly
and Stuffing Iwoud ets icecfeam Jeubaha

drink cherryade.
drinKcherryade.

Victoria Chancellor.

viCtoria chancellor

My best wish in the whole World would be to play football for ASTON VILLA I Would score loads of gools so they cold win lots of cups.

Adam

Adam French

I wish I could fly in an aeroplane I would take all my friends with me we would go to America to see the star Trec

Commander.

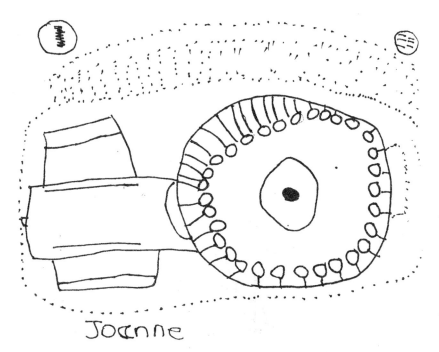

Joanne

Joanne Horsman

I WISH I
could go to
the shop and
buy some skips

Skips

by Joel

Joel Buckle

I Wish I Was in AUStralia With My Mom and My famous person Who is pamela Anderson I Wish I Could Join My favourite Rock group and Meet Meat Loaf. I Would Eat Lassagne and brink BlueBerryade

Donna Taylor

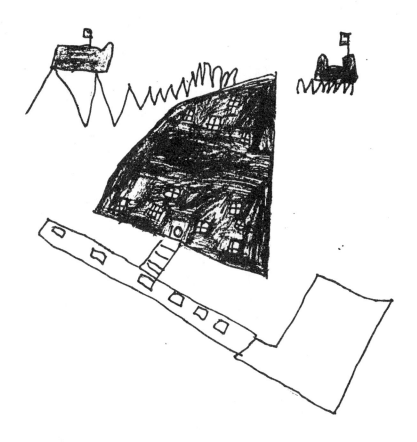

I wish I was in Germany with my mum and dad and Nathan. I wish I could meet Robson and Jerome and Cliff Richard. I would eat Chocolate teddies ice cream and German sausage. I would drink fresh orange juice.

Daniel BALDWIN

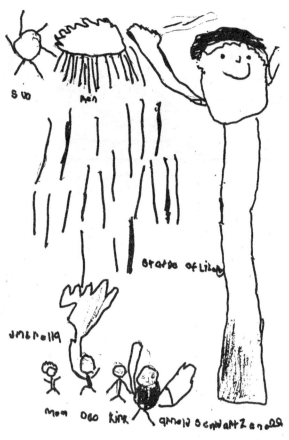

I wish   I was in America
Wien mb Mom and Dad
I would Join tne polce Force
becaose Tney have lots of gons
I wisn I could meet
arnold Gchwartzenegger

                Kirk Allen.

Our Pets

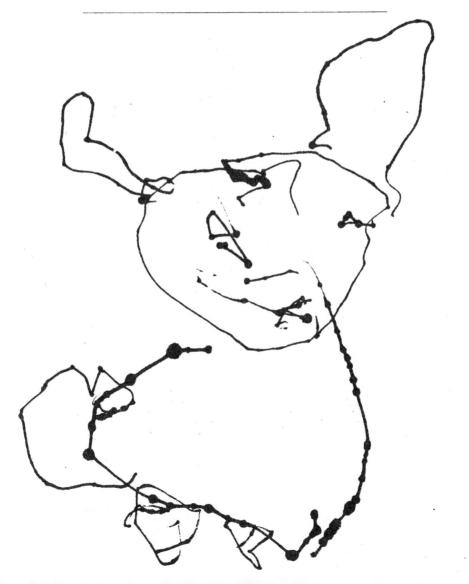

My dog goes
to sleep in
his bed.

Mark Brotherton

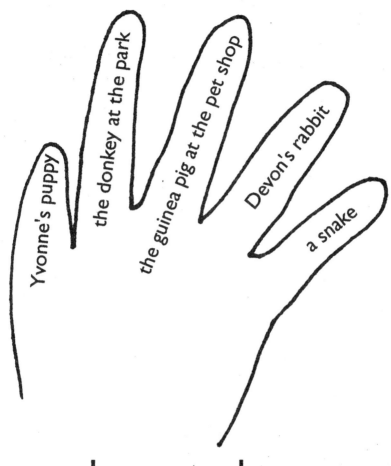

Yvonne's puppy

the donkey at the park

the guinea pig at the pet shop

Devon's rabbit

a snake

I can stroke

Sam Archer

My cat says
meow he's
got whiskers.

Emily

Emily Finlan

My cat likes to chase paper.

Chris Colder

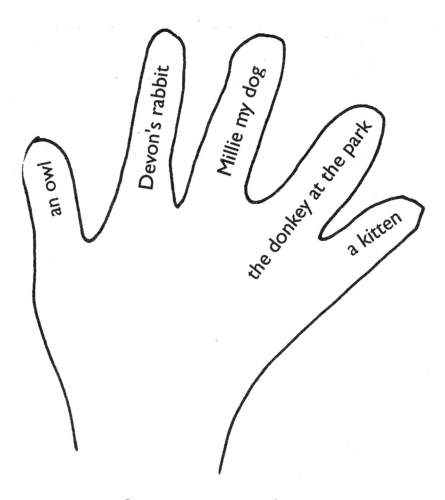

an owl

Devon's rabbit

Millie my dog

the donkey at the park

a kitten

I can stroke

Scott Gair

This is my dog Elsa
she is black and brown.
I take her for a walk
to the park.

Melissa

Melissa Mason

my dog Sam

Claire

Claire Lynes

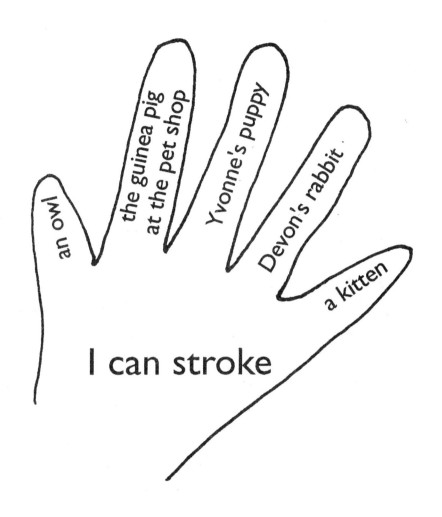

I can stroke

an owl

the guinea pig at the pet shop

Yvonne's puppy

Devon's rabbit

a kitten

Jordan Walker

Joe with his dog Kelly, she's got black hair.

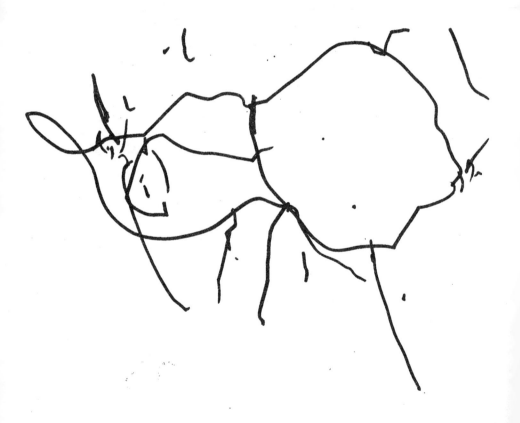

Joseph Ball

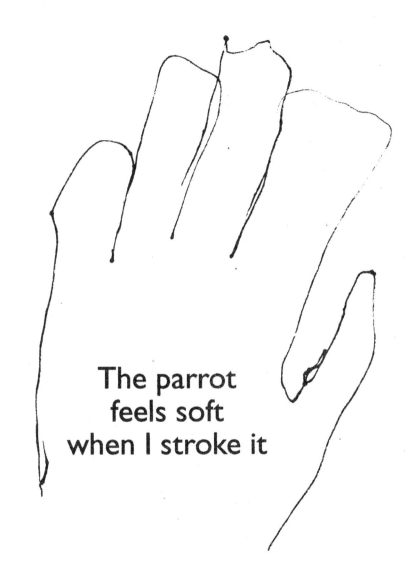

The parrot
feels soft
when I stroke it

Nicola Eager

My rabbit.

Brittany Holden

Britty

Myself

Myself

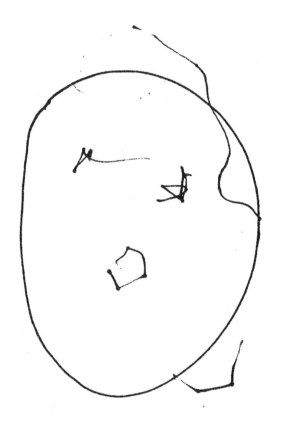

Devon White

I Like Aston Villa. They are a good. team. I Play football on the. field with my friends. I'm a. brilliant goal Keeper because. I Keep saving the ball. I listen to the footballo the radio on saturdays.

Anthony Whyte

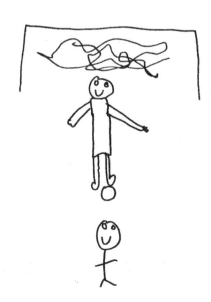

Anthony

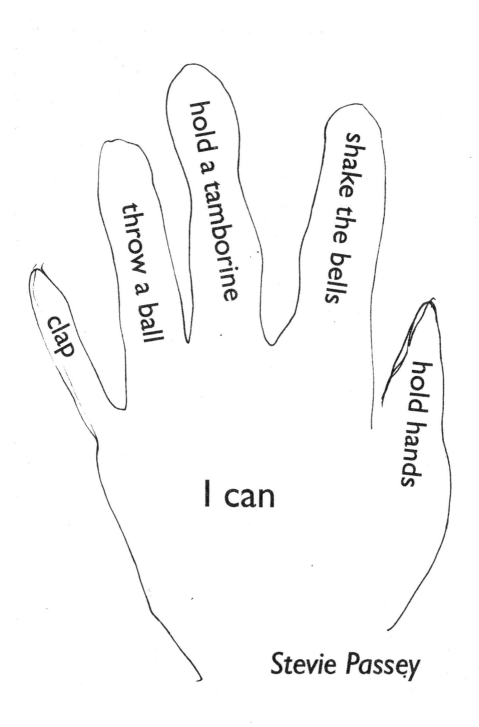

clap

throw a ball

hold a tamborine

shake the bells

hold hands

I can

Stevie Passey

Myself

Emily Noon

This is a picture of me. my name is kinstie. I like music. and swimming.

Kirstie Davies

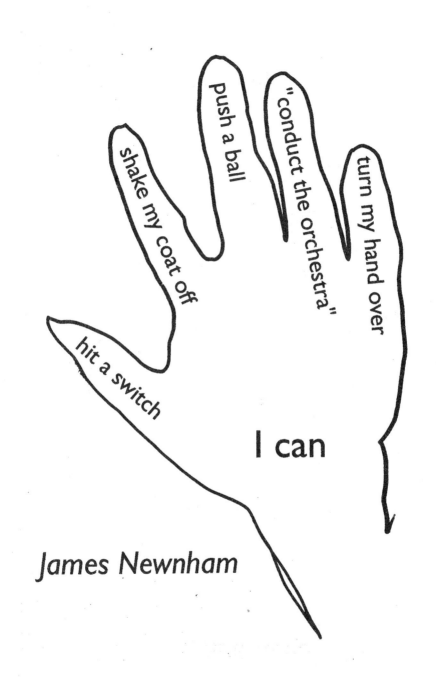

shake my coat off

push a ball

"conduct the orchestra"

turn my hand over

hit a switch

I can

James Newnham

Myself

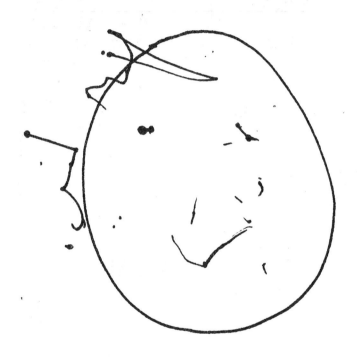

Siân Baker

my name philip
I am 15
I like going to
Stafford and visiting
the car show rooms
especially the
fiat 'Show roomg

My name is Philip, I am 15, I like going to Stafford and visiting the car showrooms especially the Fiat showrooms.

bosont fo milire
fiax

Philip Rossiter

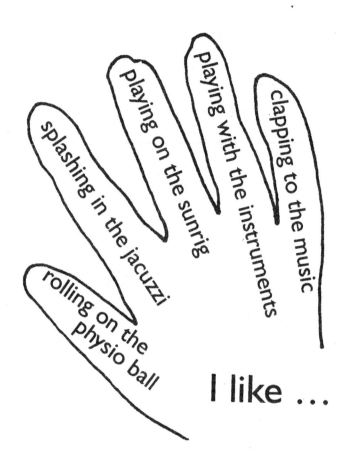

splashing in the jacuzzi

playing on the sunrig

playing with the instruments

clapping to the music

rolling on the physio ball

I like ...

Becky Jackson

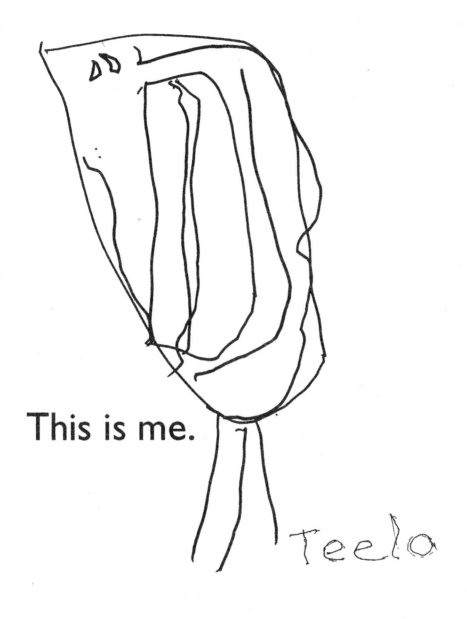

This is me.

Teela

Teela Harvey

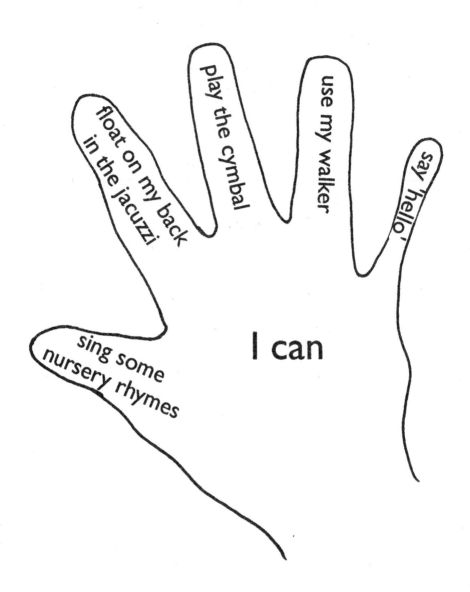

I can

float on my back
in the jacuzzi

play the cymbal

use my walker

say 'hello'

sing some
nursery rhymes

Kayleigh Carter

This is a picture of me. My name is

Felicity

Felicity Grew

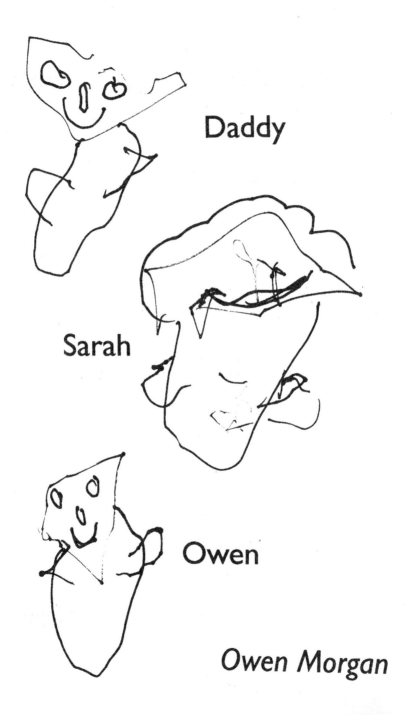

Daddy

Sarah

Owen

Owen Morgan